Classifying Living Things

Birds

Andrew Solway

Chicago, Illinois

www.heinemannraintree.com
Visit our website to find out more information about Heinemann-Raintree books.

To order:
☎ Phone 888-454-2279
💻 Visit www.heinemannraintree.com to browse our catalog and order online.

© 2003, 2009 Heinemann Library
an imprint of Capstone Global Library, LLC
Chicago, Illinois

Customer Service: 888-454-2279

Visit our website at www.heinemannraintree.com

Edited by Catherine Clarke and Claire Throp
Designed by Victoria Bevan and AMR Design, Ltd.
Original illustrations © Capstone Global Library, LLC.
Illustrations by David Woodroffe
Picture research by Hannah Taylor

Printed and bound in China by Leo Paper Group

13 12 11 10 09
10 9 8 7 6 5 4 3 2 1

Library of Congress Cataloging-in-Publication Data
Solway, Andrew.
   Classifying birds / Andrew Solway.
      p. cm. -- (Classifying living things)
Summary: Explains what birds are and how they differ from other animals, with descriptions of various types of birds, including birds of prey, water birds, and exotic birds.
Includes bibliographical references (p.   ) and index.
ISBN 978-1-4329-2353-2 (lib. bdg. : hardcover) --
ISBN 978-1-4329-2363-1 (pbk.)
   1. Birds--Classification--Juvenile literature. 2. Birds--Juvenile literature. [1. Birds.] I Title. II. Series.
   QL677 .S66 2003
   598--dc21
                                        2002015401

Acknowledgments

For Harriet, Eliza, and Nicholas.

We would like to thank the following for permission to reproduce photographs: Corbis pp. 22 (Eric and David Hosking), 25 (Francis G. Mayer); Digital Stock p. 20; © Digital Vision p. 4 (right); FLPA p. 29 (Minden Pictures/Yva Momatiuk & John Eastcott); Natural History Museum p. 27 (Michael Long); naturepl pp. 11 (John Downer), 16, 21 (John Cancalosi); Photodisc p. 5; Photolibrary pp. 4 (left), 23, 41 (OSF/Robert Tyrrell), 6 (OSF/David M Dennis), 9 (OSF/Michael Dick-AA), 12 (OSF/Mark Hamblin), 13 (OSF/Norbert Rosing), 14 (OSF/ Daniel Cox), 15 (OSF/Mary Plage), 17 (Mark Jones), 18 (Paul Souders), 19 (OSF/Doug Allen), 24 (OSF /Konrad Wothe).

Cover photograph of a pied heron riding on an Australian pelican reproduced with permission of ardea.com/Don Hadden.

We would like to thank Ann Fullick for her invaluable assistance in the preparation of this book, and Martin Lawrence for his help with the first edition.

Every effort has been made to contact copyright holders of any material reproduced in this book. Any omissions will be rectified in subsequent printings if notice is given to the publisher.

Contents

Some words are shown in bold, **like this**. You can find out what they mean by looking in the glossary.

The natural world is full of an incredible variety of **organisms**. They range from tiny bacteria, too small to see, to giant redwood trees over 100 meters (330 feet) tall. With such a bewildering variety of life, it is hard to make sense of the living world. For this reason, scientists classify living things by sorting them into groups.

Classifying the living world

Sorting organisms into groups makes them easier to understand. Scientists try to classify living things in a way that tells you how closely one group is related to another. They look at everything about an organism, from its color and shape to the **genes** inside its **cells**. They even look at **fossils** to give them clues about how living things have changed over time. Then the scientists use all this information to sort the millions of different things into groups.

Scientists do not always agree about the group an organism belongs to, so they collect as much evidence as possible to find its closest relatives.

Living things (like this humming bird and ostrich) come in all shapes and sizes.

From kingdoms to species

Classification allows us to measure the **biodiversity** of the world. To begin the classification process, scientists divide living things into huge groups called **kingdoms**. For example, plants are in one kingdom, while animals are in another. There is some argument among scientists about how many kingdoms there are—at the moment most agree that there are five! Each kingdom is then divided into smaller groups called **phyla** (singular *phylum*), and the phyla are further divided into **classes**. The next subdivision is into **orders**. Within an order, organisms are grouped into **families** and then into a **genus** (plural *genera*), which contains a number of closely related **species**. A species is a single type of organism, such as a mouse or a buttercup. Members of a species can **reproduce** and produce fertile offspring together.

Scientific names

Many living things have a common name, but these can cause confusion when the same organism has different names around the world. To avoid problems, scientists give every species a two-part Latin name, which is the same all over the world. The first part of the scientific name tells you the genus the organism belongs to. The second part tells you the exact species. Swallows, for example, have the scientific name *Hirundo rustica*, while a European swift is *Apus apus*.

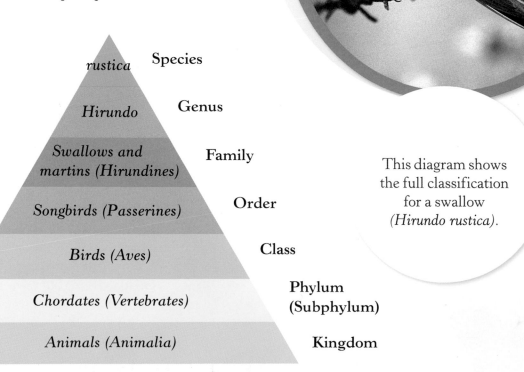

This diagram shows the full classification for a swallow (*Hirundo rustica*).

rustica	Species
Hirundo	Genus
Swallows and martins (Hirundines)	Family
Songbirds (Passerines)	Order
Birds (Aves)	Class
Chordates (Vertebrates)	Phylum (Subphylum)
Animals (Animalia)	Kingdom

How birds fit in

Birds are part of the animal **kingdom**. Animals, unlike plants, cannot make their own food and must eat other living things to stay alive. Birds are part of a group called the **vertebrates**. Like us, birds have backbones. This is what makes them vertebrates.

What makes a bird a bird?

Scientists have found several key differences between birds and other vertebrates. By looking at all the differences together, we can tell whether an animal is a bird or not.

Some vertebrates may have smooth skin, or they may be scaly or hairy. But birds are the only animals that have feathers. Most vertebrates have bony jaws, and usually teeth as well. Birds, however, all have a horny beak.

Did you know ... how animals evolve?

Over thousands or millions of years, groups of living things **evolve** (change) to fit in better with their environment (the place they live). This happens because living things that are better **adapted** (suited) to their environment live longer and produce more offspring. All the birds we see today have evolved from a single **ancestor**.

Fossils teach us about the ancestors of modern birds. This early bird, *Archaeopteryx*, lived about 150 million years ago. It had wings and feathers like a bird, but teeth and claws like a reptile.

All birds have wings. Even birds that cannot fly, such as ostriches, have small wings. Bats also have wings, but their wings are not covered with feathers. Birds are **endotherms**. This means that their bodies stay at one temperature, no matter the temperature around them, because they make their own heat. They also have very light, hollow bones.

Birds are divided into about 27 different **orders**. This table shows the main bird orders and those mentioned in this book.

Order	No. of species	Examples
Anseriformes	150	ducks, geese, and swans
Apodiformes	403	swifts and hummingbirds
Charadriiformes	257	gulls, terns, skuas, auks, snipes, sandpipers, plovers, and other shorebirds
Ciconiiformes	1,033	storks, herons, and flamingos
Columbiformes	316	pigeons, doves, and sandgrouse
Coraciiformes	193	kingfishers, bee-eaters, rollers, hornbills, and
Cuculiformes	151	cuckoos
Falconiformes	286	eagles, falcons, hawks, vultures, osprey, and secretary birds
Galliformes	256	grouse, pheasants, partridges, quails, turkeys, and jungle fowl
Gruiformes	197	cranes, rails, and bustards
Passeriformes	5,200	sparrows, starlings, robins, finches warblers, ovenbirds, tyrant flycatchers, swallows, martins, wagtails, shrikes, and thrushes
Piciformes	376	woodpeckers, jacamars, puffbirds, barbets, honeyguides, and toucans
Psittaciformes	130	parrots, cockatoos, budgerigars, lovebirds, and macaws
Strigiformes	134	owls
Struthioniformes	14	ostriches and emus

Birds are the only living things that have feathers. A bird would not be a bird without them. Feathers grow from a bird's skin in the same way that we grow hair or nails.

A bird's feathers do three important jobs:

- They give the bird a smooth, streamlined shape. This makes flying through the air easy, saving the bird's energy.
- Feathers on the bird's skinny "arms" turn them into broad, flexible wings, ideal for flying.
- Feathers on a bird's body protect its skin from the sun in hot weather and keep it warm in cold weather.

Feather structure

Feathers have a structure that makes them very light and strong. Down the center of the feather is a hollow tube, or rib. Sticking out from this rib are hundreds of thin, slanting strips called barbs. Each barb has rows of tiny teeth along its length, which link up with the teeth of the barbs on either side, like the teeth in a zipper. This locks the barbs together, making the feather into a strong, flat blade.

In wing feathers, all the barbs link together in this way. But on the body, the lower part of each feather is soft and fluffy. The fluffy (downy) part of the feather helps keep the bird warm.

This is a body feather. The enlargement shows how the teeth on each barb lock together. Each barb has lots of even tinier teeth, called barbules, on it. The barbules have "hooks" on them that zip up the barbules.

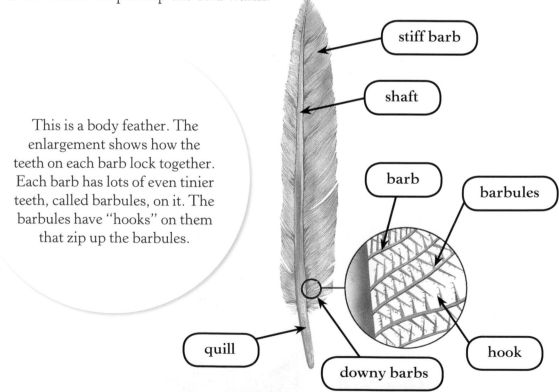

stiff barb

shaft

barb

barbules

quill

downy barbs

hook

Feathers are tough, but they must be cared for and can wear out. Birds regularly preen (clean and comb their feathers with their beak). Then about once a year, birds molt (their old feathers are replaced with new ones).

Patterns and colors

A bird's **plumage** (its feathers) can be almost any color, from dull browns and grays to bright reds and blues. The plumage may help the bird **camouflage** itself. Birds that live in reeds, for instance, often have a pattern of brown and black bars that makes them very hard to spot among the reeds.

But some birds have plumage that really stands out. They are usually male birds, and they grow brightly colored feathers to help them attract females for **breeding**. In some birds, the breeding feathers can be truly spectacular.

Wilson's bird of paradise— a beautiful show-off

- Lives in warm, tropical forests of Australia and New Guinea
- About 21 cm (8 in.) long
- Males have spectacular feathers
- Males display to attract females
- Females are brownish with a bare head

We have already seen that a bird's wing feathers help it to fly. But there is much more to flying than wings and feathers. From beak to tail, inside and out, birds are suited for flight.

Light bones

Compared to a land animal of the same size, a bird's skeleton is lighter and stronger. This helps it to fly. One way that a bird's skeleton is different is that it has fewer bones. Many of the bones in its back and pelvis (hips) are fused (joined together). A bird's wings also have fewer bones than the arms or front feet of other **vertebrates**.

A bird's beak is another **adaptation** to save weight. Jawbones and teeth are much heavier than a bird's light, strong beak. Birds have also lost their tail bones, which has helped to balance their skeleton.

In many birds, the bones themselves are lighter than those of other animals. This is because they have air spaces inside them. Bigger birds usually have more air spaces in their bones than smaller ones. A frigate bird, for example, has a wingspan of over 2 meters (6.5 feet), but its skeleton weighs less than its feathers! Even birds that have lost the ability to fly have fewer bones in their skeleton and have a beak instead of jaws.

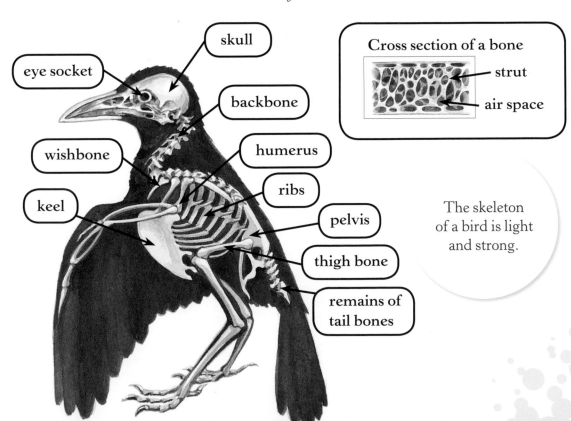

skull

eye socket

backbone

Cross section of a bone

strut

air space

wishbone

humerus

ribs

keel

pelvis

The skeleton of a bird is light and strong.

thigh bone

remains of tail bones

Strong muscles

Although birds are light, they still need a lot
of muscle power to get into the air. Nearly all
of a bird's muscles are concentrated in its body,
because heavy muscles in the wings would make
them harder to flap. The biggest muscles are the
breast muscles, which flap the wings. They are attached
to a broad, flat bone fastened to the ribs, called the keel.

Every year, bar-headed
geese fly over Mount Everest
at heights of over 9 kilometers
(5.5 miles), on their **migration**
flights. At this height there is
only one-third the amount
of oxygen in the air that
there is at sea level.

A bird's legs also need strong muscles to absorb the shock of landing.
All these muscles are concentrated at the tops of the legs—the legs
themselves are very skinny. Flightless birds have leg muscles that are
big and strong, but the muscles in the upper body are much reduced
because they do not need them for flying.

Energy for flying

Birds need a strong heart and a good blood system to keep their muscles
supplied with energy. Hummingbird hearts beat fastest of all: up to 1,200
times every minute! Human hearts beat about 70 times per minute. On
a high mountain, humans find it hard to breathe, because there is less
oxygen high in the atmosphere, but birds have no problems flying at
these heights. They have very efficient lungs, which can get more
oxygen from the air.

More than half the bird **species** in the world are passerines (perching birds). They all have feet suited for perching, with three toes pointing forward and a strong fourth toe pointing backward. Most passerines are small or medium-sized. One or two species feed in water, but most are land birds.

Although passerines have some things in common, they come in an amazing variety of colors, shapes, and sizes. Many common birds—crows, finches, sparrows, swallows, thrushes, and wrens—are passerines. The group also includes the fabulously decorated birds of paradise, **nectar**-eating sunbirds, and impressive nest-builders such as ovenbirds and weaverbirds.

Songbirds

One large group of passerines is the songbird group. All birds have short calls to keep in touch or to warn of danger. In some species, male birds have songs that they sing to mark out their territory or to attract a **mate**. But only songbirds have extra muscles in their voice box to help them sing. Not all songbirds are good singers. Few people would call the harsh croak of a crow beautiful, but crows are songbirds.

Skylark—a champion singer
- Small brown bird
- Feeds on seeds and insects
- Nests on ground
- Flies high and sings a beautiful song to identify territory

Passerine foods

Most passerines eat seeds or insects—or both. However, a few passerines eat other foods. Sunbirds are similar to hummingbirds and eat nectar from flowers. Birds of paradise eat fruit. In the tropical forests where they live, there are trees bearing fruit all year.

Nest-builders

Many passerines lay their eggs in cup-like nests or domed nests that are completely enclosed. The young are blind and helpless when they hatch. Some passerines are impressive nest-builders. Male weaver birds thread together grass and plant stems to make basket-like nests. Ovenbirds build domed clay nests, which look similar to the clay ovens that people sometimes make to cook food outdoors.

This golden pale weaver is building a nest in Mombasa, Kenya. Male weavers build nests to attract females. A female will mate with the male whose nest she likes the most.

Do you know ... how birds "chew" their food?

Birds have no teeth, so they cannot chew their food. But without chewing, it is hard for the **digestive system** to break down the food. So, birds "chew" their food in their stomachs. In many birds the food is first stored in a sac called the crop, where it is softened before going on to the gizzard. The gizzard has very tough, muscular walls. In most birds it also contains grit or small stones they have swallowed. In the gizzard the food is churned up and ground into very small pieces.

Quite a few birds live mainly on the ground—and some have even lost the ability to fly! Game birds such as pheasants, quail, and Indian jungle fowl (chicken **ancestors**) all live on the ground, although they can and do fly. On the other hand, ostriches and their relatives are flightless.

Ostriches

Ostriches, cassowaries, emus, and rheas are all large birds with long, powerful legs. Ostriches, emus, and rheas live in open country and are fast runners, while cassowaries are forest birds. They all feed mainly on plants, and they nest on the ground.

Kiwis are much smaller than their ostrich relatives and move more slowly. They hunt at night for earthworms, their favorite food. Although their eyesight is poor, they have an excellent sense of smell.

Birds like elephants!

Ostriches are the biggest living birds. They can grow up to 2.5 meters (8 feet) tall and weigh twice as much as an average man. Until a few hundred years ago in New Zealand, there were much bigger birds called moas. The biggest grew to almost 4 meters (13 feet) in height. That's taller than an elephant!

Cassowaries are nearly as big as ostriches. They have a deadly kick, and the inner nail on their feet can be 10 centimeters (4 inches) long. More people in New Guinea are killed by cassowaries than by any other wild animal.

Sage grouse—a spectacular display!

- Ground dwellers
- Nests on ground
- Males have spectacular **mating** display, called lekking, when they puff themselves up, leap, flutter, and pose to attract females

Game birds

Birds such as pheasants, grouse, partridges, and quails have for many years been bred and hunted for sport. This is why they are called "game" birds. The scientific name for them is the Galliformes. Game birds live on open ground or in forests, hunting for seeds and other plant food. They usually hide if danger threatens, but if they spot a predator (hunting animal) they suddenly burst out and fly quickly upward. A grouse can fly almost vertically from the ground.

Female game birds are usually dull-colored, but some males have splendid **plumage**. For example, the peahen has plain, brown plumage, whereas the peacock is famous for its dazzling display of colorful feathers.

Like ostriches, most game birds nest on the ground. If their young were born helpless like those of perching birds, they would soon be snapped up by predators. To avoid this, the young have feathers when they hatch and are ready to move around and feed themselves. They can fly within a day of hatching.

On rivers and streams, ponds, lakes, and marshes, you will find birds. At the water's edge, long-legged birds fish or probe for food. Farther out, other birds swim and dive. Most of these waterbirds belong to four bird **orders**: ducks and their relatives, cranes and rails, storks and herons, and pelicans.

Ducks, geese, and swans

Ducks, geese, and swans are medium-sized or large birds with webbed feet. They are good swimmers and find food by diving or "dabbling" (stretching their necks down into the water). Most of them mainly eat plants.

Ducks, geese, and swans lay their eggs in a nest on the ground. Many of them are strong fliers, and geese especially fly on long **migrations**. They often fly in a "V" formation, with each goose flying in the slipstream (current of moving air) created by the one in front. This saves energy.

Cranes and rails

Cranes and rails include some common birds, such as coots, but many birds in this group are **endangered** and could die out. They are ground-feeding or water-feeding birds. Unlike most waterbirds, they have unwebbed or slightly webbed feet, or fleshy lobes on their feet, like coots.

Swans are strong fliers, but have trouble taking off. They have to run over the water to gather speed for takeoff.

Storks, herons, and flamingos

Storks, herons, and flamingos are all long-legged birds that feed in shallow water. The group also includes spoonbills and ibises. Herons like to eat fish, which they spear using their dagger-like beak. They have a kind of "trigger" in their neck, which allows them to suddenly shoot their head forward to stab their **prey**. Flamingos feed with their heads upside down, filtering tiny creatures out of the water. Storks and their relatives use sticks to make large, messy nests in high places. In some countries they nest on the roofs of buildings.

Pelicans and their relatives

Pelicans, gannets, cormorants, and frigate birds are seabirds as well as waterbirds. Pelicans have webbing between all four toes and a pouch or sac in their throat. They use the pouch or sac as a fishing net, scooping up water and fish, then letting the water drain out. Cormorants, on the other hand, have a small throat sac that they use to cool down in hot weather. Birds in this group are mostly fish-eaters.

Most seabirds belong to one of three bird **orders**: gulls and waders, tube-nosed birds, and penguins.

Gulls and waders

This order of birds includes seabirds such as gulls and terns, shorebirds such as sandpipers and plovers, and swimming birds such as puffins and auks. They do not look similar, but they are grouped together because they have similar skulls, backbones, and voice boxes.

Terns and auks eat fish, but gulls are often scavengers, feeding on almost anything left by others. Waders feed on shores and in shallow water, digging in soft mud for worms and other creatures. Gulls and waders nest on the ground, often in a small hole scraped by the bird.

Tube-nosed birds

Tube-nosed birds include albatrosses, petrels, and shearwaters. Most animals cannot drink seawater because of the salt in it. Seabirds have glands in their nose that can remove the salt, and these glands are particularly big in tube-nosed birds. Many tube-nosed birds spend almost their whole lives feeding on the open ocean, coming to land only to **breed**.

Wandering albatross—an ocean giant

- Seabird
- Eats squid and small fish
- Largest wingspan of any living bird—average 3.1 m (10.2 ft)
- Weighs 6–12 kg (13–26 lbs)
- Spends most of its life at sea

Penguins

More than any other birds, penguins have made the sea their home. They cannot fly, and their wings have become short flippers that they use for swimming. Penguins live mostly in cold seas in the southern hemisphere (half of the world). As protection against the cold they have short, fur-like feathers and a thick layer of fat, or blubber.

Penguins come to shore mainly to breed. They usually breed in **colonies**, laying one or two eggs on a pile of stones or in a burrow. Emperor and king penguins make no nest at all. Male emperor penguins put the single egg on their feet and cover it with a special flap of skin to keep it warm.

Emperor penguins breed in the Antarctic. The female penguin lays a single egg, then returns to the sea, leaving the male to look after it. When the egg hatches two months later, the female returns to help feed the chick.

Do you know ... how far birds migrate?

Many birds **migrate** each year. They travel to find the right conditions for breeding or for winter survival. Many birds migrate long distances, but Arctic terns fly farthest of all. They spend half the year in the Arctic, then they fly across the world to the Antarctic, a one-way trip of about 16,000 kilometers (10,000 miles). Scientists are still not sure how they find their way so successfully.

Birds of **prey** are birds that catch animals or other birds for food. They have strong talons (claws) for gripping their prey and hooked beaks that are good for tearing flesh. There are two **orders**: the hawks and falcons, which mostly hunt by day, and the owls, which usually hunt by night.

Hawks and falcons

Eagles, buzzards, hawks, falcons, and Old World vultures all belong to this group of birds. Old World vultures do not usually catch their own prey—they eat carrion (dead animals). All hawks and falcons have excellent eyesight, and some vultures also have a good sense of smell.

Most hawks and falcons swoop down on their prey and grab them in their strong talons, then kill them with their sharp beaks. Some birds hunt from a perch, while others glide and soar over an area, looking for prey. Falcons dive from a height onto flying birds. They reach speeds of up to 130 kilometers (80 miles) per hour. The prey is hit so hard that the impact kills it.

Osprey—the fish eagle
- Large wing span—1.8 m (6 ft)
- Hunts fish
- Plunges talons-first into the water
- Has an extra stud on its toes for extra grip

Owls can lay up to 12 eggs. The eggs do not all hatch at once. If there is not enough food to feed all the young, the smallest ones do not get as much food. Eventually they die and are eaten by the others.

Owls

Like hawks and falcons, owls have hooked beaks and strong talons. But they look very different, with two large eyes in a round or heart-shaped face.

An owl's eyes are designed to see well in very dim light. Even more important for night hunting are an owl's ears. These are hidden under the feathers just below its eyes. The shape of the owl's face is designed to collect sounds and focus them on the ears. The ears can also tell where a sound is coming from. In territory it knows, an owl can hunt in the dark using its hearing alone.

An owl's wing-feathers have soft fringes at the tips, which soften the sound the owl makes as it flaps its wings. This means that the owl's victims do not hear it coming. It also allows the owl to hear the movements of prey animals.

Owls usually eat their prey whole. They cannot **digest** the animal's bones or fur, so after they have digested a meal, they cough up a small pellet of this undigested matter. Scientists often look at these pellets to find out what an owl has been eating.

Although many birds are talented fliers, none are more impressive than the swifts and hummingbirds. Swifts spend almost their whole life in flight, catching insects in their wide-open mouths as they fly through the air. Hummingbirds are far better than other birds at hovering in one place, and they can fly backward. Nightjars are aerial acrobats like swifts but, as their name suggests, they hunt at night.

Swifts and hummingbirds

Swifts and hummingbirds are related by their short legs and tiny feet. Some swifts have such small legs and feet that they cannot walk on flat ground.

Swifts are smallish birds with long, pointed wings. They catch insects, sleep, and even **mate** in the air. The only time they land is when they are nesting. Swifts' nests are usually high up, sometimes on the roof of a building. The nest is made from small twigs and other material, held together with saliva (spit).

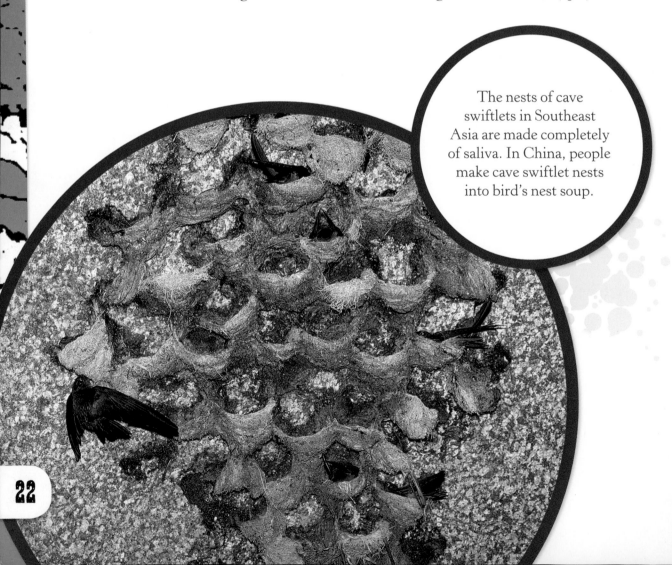

The nests of cave swiftlets in Southeast Asia are made completely of saliva. In China, people make cave swiftlet nests into bird's nest soup.

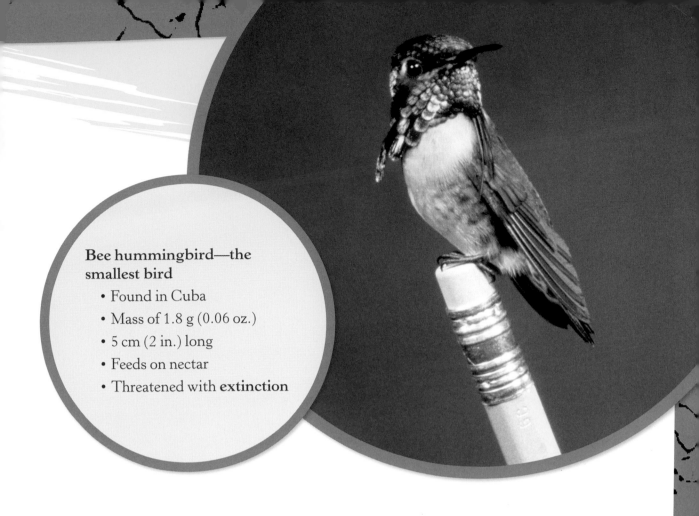

Bee hummingbird—the smallest bird
- Found in Cuba
- Mass of 1.8 g (0.06 oz.)
- 5 cm (2 in.) long
- Feeds on nectar
- Threatened with **extinction**

Hummingbirds are colorful birds with long bills. Their main food is **nectar**, which they suck from flowers with their tube-like tongues. They also eat insects. They build tiny, neat, cup-shaped nests, which they stick together with spiders' webs.

Some hummingbirds live in tropical areas where there are flowers all year, but others **migrate**. A hummingbird's wings beat very fast: up to 80 times in a second. When it hovers, the hummingbird rotates its wings as they beat, moving them in a figure-eight pattern. This is why it can hover so well.

Nightjars

Like swifts, most nightjars catch insects while in flight. They hunt mostly at night, and moths are the main food for many **species**. Nightjars have small beaks, but they can open their mouths very wide. Some species are known as frogmouths because of this. During the day, nightjars rest on the ground or in trees, relying on their excellent **camouflage** to keep them safe from enemies.

Parrots, pigeons, and cuckoos are all woodland birds, but they belong to different **orders**.

Parrots and their relatives

The parrot order includes cockatoos, budgerigars, lovebirds, and macaws. They are noisy, colorful, tropical birds that live mainly in forests. Parrots have a curved beak strong enough to crack a brazil nut, as well as strong feet that they use to help them feed and climb.

Parrots eat plant foods: seeds, fruits, nuts, and **nectar**. They often feed in large **flocks**; budgerigars feed in flocks of up to a million birds. Many **species** nest in holes, either in trees or in the ground.

Over 30 parrot species are **endangered**, many of them because their forest homes have been cut down. The kakapo is a rare New Zealand parrot that was almost wiped out by cats, which were brought to New Zealand by the first European settlers.

Pigeons and doves

Pigeons are a familiar sight in most towns and cities. They are feral, which means that they were once bred by people but then escaped into the wild. Doves and wild pigeons look similar to feral pigeons. They are mainly seed-eaters.

Parrots have often been kept as pets, because they are good at imitating human speech. Unlike most birds, they can hold food in one foot to eat it.

Pigeons build twig nests and lay one or two eggs. The young are born helpless, and at first they are fed on "pigeon milk." This is a creamy substance that the parents make in their crops (throat pouches).

Cuckoos

Cuckoos and their relatives are a varied group, but they all have a similar kind of foot. The group includes the noisy, colorful turacos and a few larger ground birds, such as the roadrunner. Cuckoos are insect-eaters. Some species specialize in eating nasty-tasting caterpillars that other animals will not eat.

About half of all cuckoo species lay their eggs in other birds' nests. The cuckoo egg hatches quickly, and the cuckoo young pushes the other baby birds out of the nest. The baby cuckoo then gets all the food that the adult birds bring to the nest.

Passenger pigeons were the most common birds ever known. Over five billion of them lived in North America. But they were good to eat, so people killed them in huge numbers. The last bird died in a zoo in 1914.

Do you know ... how baby sandgrouse drink?

Sandgrouse are desert birds related to pigeons. They have to fly long distances each day to drink. When they are first born, sandgrouse young cannot get water for themselves. So, the father bird flies to a water hole and dips his belly feathers in water. These feathers are specially designed to soak up water. He then flies back to the nest, and the young suck water from the feathers.

Is It a Bird?

Today, there are no other animals that could be confused with birds. Like birds, insects and bats can fly. But insects have no feathers or beak, and most are too small to be mistaken for birds. Bats have furry bodies and leathery wings, rather than ones made from feathers.

Millions of years ago, in the Cretaceous period (between 145 and 65 million years ago), things were not so straightforward. There were some early types of bird, such as *Archaeopteryx*, that had feathers and wings. But there were also other animals that could fly and other animals that had feathers. The other flyers were winged reptiles called pterosaurs, which had wings made from leathery skin. The feathered animals were certain **species** of dinosaur, which could not fly but were covered in feathers.

Pterosaurs

Pterosaur means "winged lizard." Pterosaurs were the first large flying animals. They first appeared when dinosaurs still roamed Earth. Their leathery wings were supported mostly by an enormously long fourth finger bone. The other three fingers formed a claw on the joint of the wing.

Rhamphorhynchus was a pterosaur. It had a long, bony tail to help it steer. The elongated fourth "finger" held the leathery wing stiff.

There were many different pterosaurs. Some had teeth and jaws like other reptiles, but some had a toothless, beak-like jaw. The biggest pterosaurs were really huge. *Quetzalcoatlus* measured 12 meters (40 feet) from wingtip to wingtip: as big as a small plane! The largest pterosaurs probably spent most of their time soaring and gliding, but the small pterosaurs could flap their wings and fly quite well.

Feathered dinosaurs

In recent years, many **fossils** of dinosaurs that have feathers have been found in China. These dinosaurs could not fly. They looked similar to small relatives of *Tyrannosaurus rex*, but with a feathery covering.

The fossils are about 125 million years old, which is several million years younger than the fossils of *Archaeopteryx*. So, these dinosaurs were living at the same time as the **ancestors** of today's flying birds.

This is an artist's idea of how *Archaeopteryx* might have looked. Unlike modern birds, *Archaeopteryx* had claws on the front of its wings. These might have helped it to climb trees.

The number of different types of living **organisms** in the world is often called **biodiversity**. Sadly, all over the world, **species** of living organisms are becoming **extinct**. This means that these organisms no longer exist on Earth. There are many different reasons for this. Extinction has always happened—some species die out and other species **evolve**. But today people are changing the world in ways that affect all other species.

People are destroying the places where animals live. We are cutting down rain forests and polluting the air and the water. Our use of fossil fuels, such as oil and gas, is causing global warming. Global warming is a rise in Earth's average temperature and a change in weather patterns. When the temperature and the weather change, it can have a serious effect on living things.

Scientists fear that around 12 percent of all bird species could be extinct within the next 100 years. That is around 1,200 types of birds that you may never be able to show your grandchildren!

This map shows how bird species are becoming increasingly threatened in Australia.

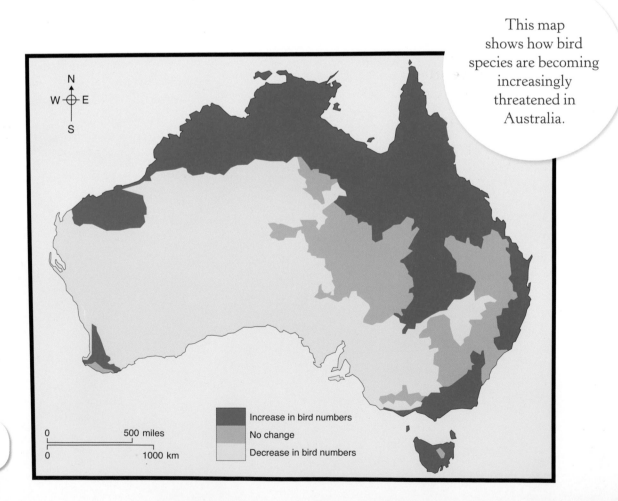

N
W ⊕ E
S

0   500 miles

0   1000 km

Increase in bird numbers

No change

Decrease in bird numbers

Some of the birds that are threatened are well known—for example, kiwis and the Californian condor. Others that are in danger, such as the purple-backed Sunbeam and the bush shrike, are less well known. Scientists think that large birds may be at more risk than smaller ones, because they often **reproduce** very slowly and there are fewer of them in the first place. Island birds are also very vulnerable.

What can be done?

To help prevent birds from becoming extinct, people need to take better care of Earth. If global warming can be stopped, many species will be saved. It is important to protect the places where birds live and **breed**. Biodiversity is important—we need as many species of birds as possible for the future.

Glossary

adaptation gradual change over many years by a living thing to fit into the place where it lives

ancestor relative from long ago

biodiversity different types of organisms around the world

breed when a male and female living thing mate and produce young

camouflage coloring and markings that blend in with the background

cell smallest unit of life

class in classification, a large grouping of living things (for example, birds) smaller than a phylum but larger than an order

colony large group of animals or plants, often of the same species, living together in a small area

digest break down food in the body

digestive system part of an animal's body (stomach, intestine, bowel) that breaks down food so that it can be absorbed into the body

endangered when an animal or plant species is in danger of dying out

endotherm animal whose body temperature stays the same because it makes its own heat

evolve change over time

extinct when a species has died out and no longer exists

family in classification, a grouping of living things (for example, gulls and terns) larger than a genus but smaller than an order

flock large gathering of birds, usually of one species

fossil remains of an ancient living creature (usually formed from bones or shells) found in rocks

gene structure by which all living things pass on characteristics to the next generation

genus (plural **genera**) in classification, a grouping of living things that is larger than a species but smaller than a family

kingdom in classification, the largest grouping of living things (for example, animals)

mate (a) verb, to create young; (b) noun, an animal's partner

migration when birds that live for part of the year in one place move to another part of the world for the rest of the year

nectar sweet liquid produced by flowers

order in classification, a grouping of living things (for example, ducks, geese, and swans) that is larger than a family but smaller than a class

organism living thing

phylum (plural **phyla**) in classification, a grouping of living things (for example, chordates) that is larger than an order but smaller than a kingdom

plumage bird's feathers

prey animal that is hunted for food by another animal

reproduce give birth to babies

species in classification, the smallest grouping of living things (for example, herring gulls) that are all similar and can reproduce together

vertebrates animals with backbones

Find Out More

Books

Doherty, Gillian. *Birds*. Tulsa, Okla.: EDC, 2001.

Pyers, Greg. *Classifying Animals: Why Am I a Bird?* Chicago: Raintree, 2006.

Snedden, Robert. *Living Things: Birds*. Mankato, Minn.: Smart Apple Media, 2009.

Stefoff, Rebecca. *Family Trees: The Bird Class*. Tarrytown, N.Y.: Marshall Cavendish, 2007.

Websites

http://kids.yahoo.com/animals/birds
On this web page there are lots of links to information about individual birds.

http://nationalzoo.si.edu/Animals/Birds/ForKids/default.cfm
This web page has fact sheets and games about all kinds of birds.

www.fws.gov/birds
This is the section about birds within the U.S. Fish and Wildlife Service website.

www.npwrc.usgs.gov/resource/birds/chekbird/
This map provided by the U.S. Geological Survey shows which kinds of birds live in different parts of the United States.

www.mnh.si.edu
This is the website of the National Museum of Natural History in Washington, D.C.

Index